Johann Nepomuk Humme

MASS IN B♭

Vocal Score / *Klavierauszug*

Edited by / *Herausgegeben von*
JOHN ERIC FLOREEN

Music Department
OXFORD UNIVERSITY PRESS
New York and Oxford

A recording of the Mass in B flat is available from Spectrum, a division of Uni-Pro Recordings, Harriman, NY 10926. The work is performed by Westminster Choir College Oratorio Choir and the New Brunswick Chamber Orchestra, under the direction of John Eric Floreen.

CONTENTS · *INHALT*

PREFACE

Johann Nepomuk Hummel (b. 1778, Pressburg [now Bratislava, Czechoslovakia]; d. 1837, Weimar) was one of the key figures of late Viennese Classicism. A student of Mozart, Haydn, and Salieri, and a friend of Goethe, in his time he was regarded as one of Europe's greatest pianists and as a composer second only to Beethoven.

Hummel wrote most of his choral music while serving as Haydn's successor as Konzertmeister to the Esterházy family at Eisenstadt from 1804 to 1811. His considerable output includes five symphonic masses, a Te Deum, cantatas, offertories, partsongs, and an oratorio.

The Mass in B flat was dedicated to Prince Nikolaus Esterházy II, and was intended for performance at the court on the Prince's name-day. The autograph score, which bears the title *Missa da Sti. Nicolaii* (later crossed out), is dated 10 November 1810. According to court records, however, a Mass in B flat was performed in 1805 under Hummel's direction in the Eisenstadt parish church (now the cathedral), suggesting that the work may have been begun soon after his arrival at the Esterházy court.

In 1818 S. A. Steiner of Vienna published the first edition of the work, which bore a dedication to Hummel's employer at that time, the King of Württemberg. In a second edition, published in Vienna c.1830 by Steiner's successor, Tobias Haslinger, the dedication was again changed, this time to honour the King of Saxony. Both editions were evidently issued under the composer's supervision.

The Mass in B flat is scored for SATB chorus (there are no vocal solos) and a modest orchestra consisting of 2 oboes, 2 bassoons, 2 trumpets, timpani, strings, and organ continuo. Two clarinet parts are included with the Eisenstadt set of parts, and a note in Hummel's hand on their covers indicates that they may be used in place of oboes ('Statt der Oboe kann es auf Clarinet zur Abwechslung gespielt werden').

A reduced instrumentation, in which some or all of the wind instrument lines may be played by the organ, was provided by the publisher in the first edition. The organ part includes sections from the most prominent oboe, bassoon, and trumpet passages, which appear above the figured bass. These were to be played by the organist if wind instruments were not available ('In Ermanglung der Blasinstrumente sind selbe auf der Orgel zu spielen'). The practice of adjusting the instrumentation of symphonic masses to local exigencies in this way was common during the late eighteenth and early nineteenth centuries in and around Vienna, as well as in other parts of the old Austrian–Habsburg Empire and South Germany. A well-known example is the original instrumentation of Haydn's 'Nelson' Mass (1798), although in this case the organ part was composed first and the woodwind lines supplied later by Johann Nepomuk Fuchs.

The organ part for this edition of the Mass in B flat (included with the set of rental parts) comprises the editor's realization of the figured bass and the optional wind passages. Consequently this work can be performed with forces as small as string quartet, double bass, organ, and chorus; these can be augmented by the trumpets and timpani and/or the woodwind, as available. The rental full score is a photo-reproduction of the Haslinger edition full score (1830). The orchestral parts (except for the organ and clarinet parts) are photo-reproductions of the Steiner edition (1818).

The sources for this work are: (*a*) an autograph preserved in the Deutsche Staatsbibliothek, East Berlin (Mus. ms. autogr. 4 J. N. Hummel); (*b*) a set of manuscript parts preserved in a private archive in Eisenstadt (including an organ part largely in Hummel's hand); (*c*) the Steiner edition (full score and parts); and (*d*) the Haslinger edition (full score).

All dynamic, phrase, articulation, and tempo marks in this edition are the composer's, as well as the metronome marks at the beginning of each movement or section.

The editor gratefully acknowledges the Hummel Classical Foundation's assistance in making available a set of the Steiner orchestral parts. Thanks are also due to Wolfgang Goldhan (Deutsche Staatsbibliothek), J. Kenneth Wilson (Rutgers University, Newark), and Martin Haselböck (Vienna). Work on this edition has been generously aided by two Fulbright Awards for research in Austria as well as by support from the Hummel Classical Foundation, the American Philosophical Society, the National Endowment for the Humanities, the International Research and Exchanges Board, the Deutsche Akademische Austauschdienst, and the Rutgers University Research Council.

JOHN ERIC FLOREEN
*Rutgers—The State University of
New Jersey Campus at Newark
June 1987*

VORWORT

Johann Nepomuk Hummel (geb. 1778 in Pressburg [heute Bratislava, Tschechoslowakei]; gest. 1837 in Weimar) war eine der Schlüsselfiguren der späten Wiener Klassik. Er war Schüler Mozarts, Haydns und Salieris und mit Goethe befreundet. Zu seiner Zeit hielt man ihn für einen der größten Pianisten Europas und als Komponisten nur Beethoven nachstehend.

Hummel schrieb den größten Teil seiner Chorwerke in der Zeit, als er – als Nachfolger Haydns – bei der Familie Esterházy als Konzertmeister engagiert war; das war von 1804 bis 1811. Seine beträchtliche Produktion umfaßt unter anderem fünf symphonische Messen, ein Te Deum, Kantaten, Offertorien, mehrstimmige Lieder und ein Oratorium.

Die Messe in B-Dur ist dem Fürsten Nikolaus Esterházy I gewidmet und war gedacht für eine Aufführung bei Hofe am Namenstag des Fürsten. Die autographe Partitur trägt den Titel *Missa da Sti. Nicolaii* (später durchgestrichen) und das Datum 10. November 1810. Jedoch wurde nach Aufzeichnungen aus dem Fürstenhause eine Messe in B-Dur schon 1805 aufgeführt, und zwar unter Hummels Leitung und in der Eisenstädter Pfarrkirche (heute Kathedrale); es kann also sein, daß Hummel gleich nach seiner Ankunft am Esterházyschen Hofe mit der Arbeit begann.

1818 veröffentlichte S. A. Steiner aus Wien das Werk zum ersten Mal; da trug die Ausgabe eine Widmung an Hummels Arbeitgeber zu jener Zeit, den König von Württemberg. In einer zweiten Ausgabe, erschienen um 1830 in Wien bei Steiners Nachfolger Tobias Haslinger, war die Zueignung wiederum verändert, diesmal galt sie dem König von Sachsen. Beide Ausgaben sind offensichtlich unter Beaufsichtigung durch den Komponisten herausgekommen.

Die Messe in B-Dur erfordert vierstimmigen gemischten Chor, keine Vokalsoli und ein bescheidenes Orchester aus 2 Oboen, 2 Fagotten, 2 Trompeten, Pauken, Streichern und Orgelcontinuo. Der Eisenstädter Stimmensatz enthält auch zwei Klarinettenstimmen; eine Bemerkung auf dem Umschlag von Hummels eigener Hand weist darauf hin, daß diese Stimmen als Alternative zur Oboenbesetzung verwendet werden sollten („Statt der Oboe kann es auf Clarinet zur Abwechslung gespielt werden").

Der Herausgeber der ersten Ausgabe hat eine ausgezogene Fassung erstellt, in der einige oder alle Blasinstrumentenpartien von der Orgel übernommen werden können. Die Orgelstimme enthält die wichtigsten Oboen-, Fagott- und Trompetenpassagen, die über dem bezifferten Baß erscheinen. Die Fassung war für den Fall gedacht, daß Blasinstrumentalisten nicht zu haben waren. („In Ermanglung der Blasinstrumente sind selbe auf der Orgel zu spielen.") Die Praxis, die Instrumentation symphonischer Messen an die örtlichen Gegebenheiten anzupassen, war im späten 18. und frühen 19. Jahrhundert in und um Wien ebenso wie in anderen Teilen des alten Österreichisch-Habsburgischen Reiches und in Süddeutschland gang und gäbe. Ein sehr bekanntes Beispiel dafür ist Haydns „Nelson"-Messe (1798), wenn auch in diesem Fall zuerst der Orgelpart komponiert und die Blasinstrumentenstimmen später von Johann Nepomuk Fuchs ergänzt wurden.

Die Orgelstimme der vorliegenden Ausgabe der B-Dur-Messe (zusammen mit den anderen Stimmen als Leihmaterial erhältlich) enthält die Generalbaßaussetzung des Herausgebers einschließlich der ggf. zu übernehmenden Bläserpassagen. Infolgedessen kann das Werk mit einer minimalen Besetzung aus Streichquartett, Kontrabaß, Orgel und Chor ausgeführt werden; diese Besetzung kann natürlich erweitert werden durch Trompeten und Pauken und/oder Holzbläser, je nach Verfügbarkeit. Die Leihpartitur ist eine photographische Wiedergabe der Haslinger-Ausgabe von *c.*1830. Die Orchesterstimmen (außer der Orgelstimme und den Klarinettenstimmen) sind eine photographische Wiedergabe der Steiner-Ausgabe von 1818.

Für das vorliegende Werk gibt es folgende Quellen: (*a*) Autograph, verwahrt in der Deutschen Staatsbibliothek in Berlin, DDR (Mus. ms. autogr. 4 J. N. Hummel); (*b*) ein handgeschriebener Stimmensatz in einem privaten Archiv in Eisenstadt (dabei eine Orgelstimme, die weitgehend von Hummels Hand stammt); (*c*) die Steiner-Ausgabe (vollständige Partitur und Stimmen); (*d*) die Haslinger-Ausgabe (vollständige Partitur).

Alle Angaben zu Dynamik, Phrasierung, Artikulation und Tempo in der Ausgabe stammen vom Komponisten, ebenso die Metronomangaben am Beginn jedes Satzes oder Abschnitts.

Der Herausgeber dankt der Hummel Classical Foundation, die bei der Beschaffung eines Orchesterstimmensatzes der Steiner-Ausgabe behilflich war. Dank schuldet er ebenso Wolfgang Goldhan (Deutsche Staatsbibliothek), J. Kenneth Wilson (Rutgers University, Newark) und Martin Haselböck (Wien). Die Arbeit an dieser Ausgabe wurde großzügig unterstützt durch zwei Fulbright-Stipendien für Forschungen in Österreich sowie durch die Hummel Classical Foundation, die American Philosophical Society, die National Endowment for the Humanities, das International Research and Exchanges Board, den Deutschen Akademischen Austauschdienst und den Rutgers University Research Council.

Übersetzung:
Cornelia Eichberg

JOHN ERIC FLOREEN
Rutgers—The State University of New Jersey Campus at Newark
Juni 1987

INSTRUMENTATION

2 oboes (or 2 clarinets in B flat)*

2 bassoons*

2 trumpets*

timpani*

strings

organ continuo

SATB chorus

*Optional (see Preface)

Full scores and orchestral material are available on rental from the publisher.

Duration: *c*.35 minutes

MASS IN B♭
Op. 77

Edited by
John Eric Floreen

KYRIE

JOHANN NEPOMUK HUMMEL
(1778–1837)

Printed in Great Britain

OXFORD UNIVERSITY PRESS, MUSIC DEPARTMENT WALTON STREET, OXFORD, OX2 6DP

2

3

8

GLORIA

9

12

Qui tollis

18

Quoniam

Tempo primo

Quo - ni-am tu so - lus san - ctus, tu so-lus Do - mi-nus, tu so - lus Al-

Quo - ni-am tu so - lus san - ctus, tu so-lus Do - mi-nus, tu so - lus Al-

Quo - ni-am tu so - lus san - ctus, tu so-lus Do - mi-nus, tu so - lus Al-

Quo - ni-am tu so - lus san - ctus, tu so-lus Do - mi-nus, tu so - lus Al-

Tempo primo

tis - si-mus, Je - su Chri - ste.

tis - si-mus, Je - su Chri - ste.

tis - si-mus, Je - su Chri - ste.

tis - si-mus, Je - su Chri - ste.

24

28

CREDO

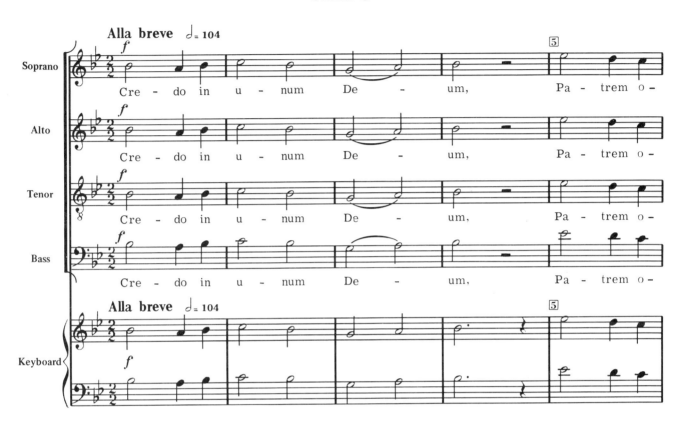

32

42

44

47

48

52

SANCTUS

53

54

BENEDICTUS

58

62

AGNUS DEI

Dona nobis

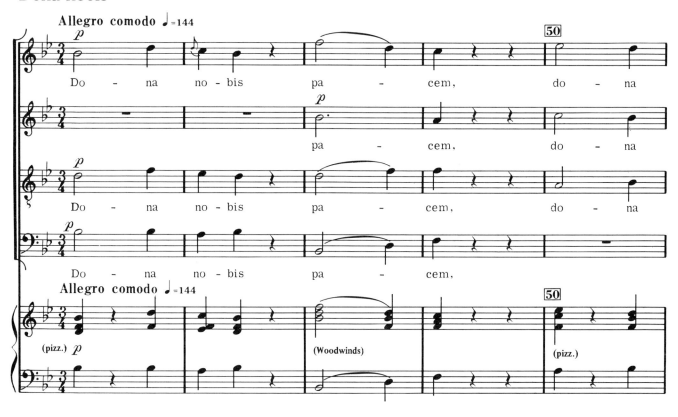